# Immigration to the United States

# German Immigrants

*Lisa Trumbauer*

*Robert Asher, Ph.D., General Editor*

Facts On File, Inc.

**Immigration to the United States: German Immigrants**

Facts On File, Inc.
132 West 31st Street
New York NY 10001

**Library of Congress Cataloging-in-Publication Data**
Trumbauer, Lisa, 1963-
  German immigrants / Lisa Trumbauer.
    p. cm. – (Immigration to the United States)
  Includes bibliographical references and index.
  ISBN 0-8160-5683-8 (alk. paper)
  1. German Americans–History–Juvenile literature. 2.  Immigrants–United States–
  History–Juvenile literature. 3.  German Americans–Juvenile literature.  I. Title. II. Series.
  E184.G3T78 2005
  973'.0431–dc22

                                                                    2004017849

Facts On File books are available at special discounts when purchased in bulk quantities for businesses, associations, institutions, or sales promotions. Please call our Special Sales Department in New York at (212) 967-8800 or (800) 322-8755.

You can find Facts On File on the World Wide Web at http://www.factsonfile.com

Cover design by Cathy Rincon
A Creative Media Applications Production
Interior design: Fabia Wargin & Luís Leon
Editor: Laura Walsh
Copy editor: Laurie Lieb
Proofreader: Tania Bissell
Photo researcher: Jennifer Bright

Photo Credits:
p. 1 © Bettmann/CORBIS; p. 4 © The Historical Society of Pennsylvania (HSP); p. 11 © Getty Images/Hulton Archive; p. 15 © Time Life Pictures/Getty Images; p. 17 © Bettmann/CORBIS; p. 20 © The Historical Society of Pennsylvania (HSP); p. 23 © North Wind Archives; p. 25 © The Historical Society of Pennsylvania (HSP); p. 26 © North Wind Archives; p. 30 © The Library of Congress; p. 34 © The Granger Collection, New York; p. 35 © North Wind Archives; p. 37 © Eureka Pioneer Museum of McPherson County; p. 39 © Bettmann/CORBIS; p. 40 © Bettmann/CORBIS; p. 42 © Bettmann/CORBIS; p. 46 © Bettmann/CORBIS; p. 48 © Bettmann/CORBIS; p. 51 © The Library of Congress; p. 52 © The Library of Congress; p. 53 © North Wind Archives; p. 55 © Eureka Pioneer Museum of McPherson County; p. 60 © Bettmann/CORBIS; p. 61 © AP Photo; p. 63 © Bettmann/CORBIS; p. 65 © Bettmann/CORBIS; p. 67 © Bettmann/CORBIS; p. 71 © AP Photo; p. 72 © Bettmann/CORBIS; p. 75 © Bettmann/CORBIS; p. 78 Courtesy Ellis Island Immigration Museum; p. 82 © Bettmann/CORBIS; p. 84 © AP Photo/Rob Schoenbaum; p. 89 © Jim Sugar/CORBIS

Printed in the United States of America

VH PKG  10 9 8 7 6 5 4 3 2 1

This book is printed on acid-free paper.

Previous page: *The Klaus family from Mannheim, Germany, is sworn in and registered as German immigrants at the General Post Office in New York City in 1940.*

# Contents

# A Nation
# of Immigrants

*Robert Asher,* Ph.D.

*Left: Quakers arrived from England in the colony of Pennsylvania in the 1600s pulled by the idea of religious freedom and tolerance. Their diversity and ideals helped shape the future of the United States.*

Human beings have always moved from one place to another. Sometimes they have sought territory with more food or better economic conditions. Sometimes they have moved to escape poverty or been forced to flee from invaders who have taken over their territory. When people leave one country or region to settle in another, their movement is called emigration. When people come into a new country or region to settle, it is called immigration. The new arrivals are called immigrants.

People move from their home country to settle in a new land for two underlying reasons. The first reason is that negative conditions in their native land push them to leave. These are called "push factors." People are pushed to emigrate from their native land or region by such things as poverty, religious persecution, or political oppression.

The second reason that people emigrate is that positive conditions in the new country pull them to the new land. These are called "pull factors." People immigrate to new countries seeking opportunities that do not exist in their native country. Push and pull factors often work together. People leave poor conditions in one country seeking better conditions in another.

Sometimes people are forced to flee their homeland because of extreme hardship, war, or oppression. These immigrants to new lands are called refugees. During times of war or famine, large groups of refugees may immigrate to new countries in

search of better conditions. Refugees have been on the move
from the earliest recorded history. Even today, groups of
refugees are forced to move from one country to another.

# Pulled to America

For hundreds of years, people have been pulled to America
seeking freedom and economic opportunity. America has
always been a land of immigrants. The original settlers of
America emigrated from Asia thousands of years ago. These first
Americans were probably following animal herds in search of
better hunting grounds. They migrated to America across a land
bridge that connected the west coast of North America with
Asia. As time passed, they spread throughout North and South
America and established complex societies and cultures.

Beginning in the 1500s, a new group of immigrants came
to America from Europe. The first European immigrants to
America were volunteer sailors and soldiers who were promised
rewards for their labor. Once settlements were established, small
numbers of immigrants from Spain, Portugal, France, Holland,
and England began to arrive. Some were rich, but most were
poor. Most of these emigrants had to pay for the expensive
ocean voyage from Europe to the Western Hemisphere by
promising to work for four to seven years. They were called
indentured servants. These emigrants were pushed out of
Europe by religious persecution, high land prices, and poverty.
They were pulled to America by reports of cheap, fertile land
and by the promise of more religious freedom than they had in
their homelands.

Many immigrants who arrived in America, however, did
not come by choice. Convicts were forcibly transported from
England to work in the American colonies. In addition,

thousands of African men, women, and children were kidnapped in Africa and forced onto slave ships. They were transported to America and forced to work for European masters. While voluntary emigrants had some choice of which territory they would move to, involuntary immigrants had no choice at all. Slaves were forced to immigrate to America from the 1500s until about 1840. For voluntary immigrants, two things influenced where they settled once they arrived in the United States. First, immigrants usually settled where there were jobs. Second, they often settled in the same places as immigrants who had come before them, especially those who were relatives or who had come from the same village or town in their homeland. This is called chain migration. Immigrants felt more comfortable living among people whose language they understood and whom they might have known in the "old country."

Immigrants often came to America with particular skills that they had learned in their native countries. These included occupations such as carpentry, butchering, jewelry making, metal machining, and farming. Immigrants settled in places where they could find jobs using these skills.

In addition to skills, immigrant groups brought their languages, religions, and customs with them to the new land. Each of these many cultures has made unique contributions to American life. Each group has added to the multicultural society that is America today.

# Waves of Immigration

Many immigrant groups came to America in waves. In the early 1800s, economic conditions in Europe were growing harsh. Famine in Ireland led to a massive push of emigration of Irish men and women to the United States. A similar number of

German farmers and urban workers migrated to America. They were attracted by high wages, a growing number of jobs, and low land prices. Starting in 1880, huge numbers of people in southern and eastern Europe, including Italians, Russians, Poles, and Greeks, were facing rising populations and poor economies. To escape these conditions, they chose to immigrate to the United States. In the first 10 years of the 20th century, immigration from Europe was in the millions each year, with a peak of 8 million immigrants in 1910. In the 1930s, thousands of Jewish immigrants fled religious persecution in Nazi Germany and came to America.

# Becoming a Legal Immigrant

There were few limits on the number of immigrants that could come to America until 1924. That year, Congress limited immigration to the United States to only 100,000 per year. In 1965, the number of immigrants allowed into the United States each year was raised from 100,000 to 290,000. In 1986, Congress further relaxed immigration rules, especially for immigrants from Cuba and Haiti. The new law allowed 1.5 million legal immigrants to enter the United States in 1990. Since then, more than half a million people have legally immigrated to the United States each year.

Not everyone who wants to immigrate to the United States is allowed to do so. The number of people from other countries who may immigrate to America is determined by a federal law called the Immigration and Naturalization Act (INA). This law was first passed in 1952. It has been amended (changed) many times since then.

Following the terrorist attacks on the World Trade Center in
New York City and the Pentagon in Washington, D.C., in 2001,
Congress made significant changes in the INA. One important
change was to make the agency that administers laws concerning
immigrants and other people entering the United States part of
the Department of Homeland Security (DHS). The DHS is
responsible for protecting the United States from attacks by terror-
ists. The new immigration agency is called the Citizenship and
Immigration Service (CIS). It replaced the previous agency, which
was called the Immigration and Naturalization Service (INS).

When noncitizens enter the United States, they must
obtain official permission from the government to stay in the
country. This permission is called a visa. Visas are issued by the
CIS for a specific time period. In order to remain in the
country permanently, an immigrant must obtain a permanent
resident visa, also called a green card. This document allows a
person to live, work, and study in the United States for an
unlimited amount of time.

To qualify for a green card, an immigrant must have a
sponsor. In most cases, a sponsor is a member of the immigrant's family who is a U.S. citizen or holds a green card. The
government sets an annual limit of 226,000 on the number of
family members who may be sponsored for permanent residence. In addition, no more than 25,650 immigrants may come
from any one country.

In addition to family members, there are two other main
avenues to obtaining a green card. A person may be sponsored
by a U.S. employer or may enter the Green Card Lottery. An
employer may sponsor a person who has unique work qualifica-
tions. The Green Card Lottery randomly selects 50,000 winners
each year to receive green cards. Applicants for the lottery may
be from any country from which immigration is allowed by
U.S. law.

However, a green card does not grant an immigrant U.S. citizenship. Many immigrants have chosen to become citizens of the United States. Legal immigrants who have lived in the United States for at least five years and who meet other requirements may apply to become naturalized citizens. Once these immigrants qualify for citizenship, they become full-fledged citizens and have all the rights, privileges, and obligations of other U.S. citizens.

Even with these newer laws, there are always more people who want to immigrate to the United States than are allowed by law. As a result, some people choose to come to the United States illegally. Illegal immigrants do not have permission from the U.S. government to enter the country. Since 1980, the number of illegal immigrants entering the United States, especially from Central and South America, has increased greatly. These illegal immigrants are pushed by poverty in their homelands and pulled by the hope of a better life in the United States. Illegal immigration cannot be exactly measured, but it is believed that between 1 million and 3 million illegal immigrants enter the United States each year.

This series, Immigration to the United States, describes the history of the immigrant groups that have come to the United States. Some came because of the pull of America and the hope of a better life. Others were pushed out of their homelands. Still others were forced to immigrate as slaves. Whatever the reasons for their arrival, each group has a unique story and has made a unique contribution to the American way of life. ❋

Right:
*A painting by artist Ben Shahn depicts Albert Einstein, a great German scientist, leading a group of fellow immigrants into an American internment camp during World War II. The U.S. government feared that immigrants could pose a security risk. (Einstein was not actually interned.)*

# Introduction

# German Immigration

*Seeking a Better Life*

**O**n October 3, 2003, the president of the United States, George W. Bush, made this statement:

> *As one of the largest ethnic groups in the United States, German Americans have greatly influenced our country in the fields of business, government, law, science, athletics, the arts, and many others. . . . In addition to their many professional achievements, German Americans have influenced American culture. From Christmas trees to kindergartens, the United States has adopted many German traditions and institutions. By celebrating and sharing their customs and traditions, German Americans help to preserve their rich heritage and enhance the cultural diversity of the Nation.*

The president's statement went on to read: "Now, therefore, I, George W. Bush, President of the United States of America, by virtue of the authority vested in me by the Constitution and laws of the United States, do hereby proclaim October 6, 2003, as German-American Day. I encourage all Americans to recognize the contributions to the liberty and prosperity of the United States of our citizens of German descent."

The first group of German immigrants arrived in America on that date, October 6, in 1683. Now, more than 300 years later, about 60 million Americans claim to have German ancestors. That is about one-fourth the population of the United States. In fact, German immigrants became the first non-English-speaking group whose population was larger than that of English-speaking immigrants.

With so many German immigrants coming to the United States and Canada, it was only natural that many aspects of German life would become part of American culture. When German immigrants began decorating trees during Christmastime, which was the custom in Germany, many Americans also did so. German schools for young children, called *kindergartens,* soon became part of most elementary schools. And all Americans enjoyed German food and drink, especially German sausages (frankfurters, or hot dogs) and ground-beef steaks called hamburgers.

Individual German Americans also left their mark on the United States. Henry Steinway crafted beautiful pianos in the 1800s. Milton Hershey, whose ancestors arrived in America in the 1700s, created the famous Hershey chocolate factory. And Albert Einstein was one of the most brilliant scientists of the twentieth century.

Like many immigrant groups, Germans who came to America were looking for a better way of life. Some may have been looking for religious or political freedom. Many others came to the United States to look for work and a stable future for their families. Exploring the story of German immigration is a window into both America's own past and Germany's past as well.

# Germany on the Map

On a world map, Germany sits right in the middle of Europe. It is bordered by the countries of the Netherlands, Belgium, Luxembourg, and France to the west. Poland and the Czech Republic border Germany to the east. Austria and Switzerland are at Germany's southern border. To the north, Germany is bordered by the North Sea and the Baltic Sea, as well as the country of Denmark.

During the last centuries, these borders have changed, mostly during times of war. As recently as the 1980s, Germany was shown on a map as two countries—West Germany and East Germany. The two countries were unified (brought together as one country) in 1990. A map of Europe from the early 1800s does not show a country named Germany at all. Before 1871, what is today known as Germany was a collection of more than 200 states, called principalities. It was not until 1871 that these states were united as one country called Germany.

Throughout the centuries, there have been many conflicts in Germany. One of the most important conflicts was about religion. This conflict led to a time known as the Reformation, when the Protestant religions developed. Events during the Reformation caused many Germans to search for a new homeland, where they would not be punished for their religious beliefs.

## An Important Invention

Before the 1400s, most books were created by writing the text by hand. In the mid-1400s, a German named Johannes Gutenberg invented what many consider to be the first printing press with movable type in Europe. (Movable type was blocks carved with individual words or letters that could be moved around on the printing press to make different sentences.) This invention was important because books could now be printed in larger quantities. The first book to be made on the printing press was the Bible. At that time, the Bible was written in Latin. Soon the Bible was translated into German. Now, more people could read the Bible, not just church officials. As more people read the Bible, more interpretations of its meanings could be made.

# A Step Back in Time

In the 1400s, Germany was made up of more than 200 states. These states were considered German, but not because they were part of a country called Germany. They were considered German because the people who lived there spoke the same language and had similar customs and heritages.

Because they were separate states, each had its own ruler. These rulers were mostly princes or other high-ranking members of society. The rulers had complete control over their states, and they often raised taxes on the common people who lived there. Many of these rulers abused their power. This became a growing problem.

As the centuries passed, another problem arose. The pope, the leader of the Roman Catholic Church, became very powerful. The church constantly asked the people for money. People were unhappy with the church because of this demand. The common people became poorer while the church became richer, yet it did not pay taxes, as normal citizens did.

In 1517, a German friar named Martin Luther (1483–1546) spoke out against the Roman Catholic Church. He believed that the Bible should be open to interpretation. In other words, he felt that each person who read the Bible should be able to find his or her own meanings in the words. Luther also believed that one central controlling organization, such as the Roman Catholic Church, had no right to tell others how to worship.

The Roman Catholic Church was not pleased with Martin Luther's theories. However, many people were tired of giving money to the church. They were also tired of following the religious rules set by church officials. They agreed with Luther's theories, and Luther gained many followers. This religious movement became known as the Reformation, when the Protestant religions were born.

Martin Luther believed that people should feel free to worship however they chose. This belief led to the creation of several different Protestant religions, such as the Lutherans, the Reformed (also called the Calvinists), and the Mennonites. The Reformation affected not only mainland Europe, but Great Britain as well. There, the Quaker faith took root.

The conflict between the Catholic and Protestant religions continued for many decades. It finally ended in a war that lasted thirty years.

*Martin Luther, German-born leader of the Reformation, is shown in this 16th-century portrait.*

# The Thirty Years' War

The Thirty Years' War was fought between 1618 and 1648. Although the war involved all of Europe, the battles were fought mostly on German lands. The war was fought mostly between two groups. One was made up of German Protestant princes and their allies, including the countries of France, Sweden, Denmark, and England. The other group was the Catholic Holy Roman Empire. It included Austria, Spain, Bohemia (a region that is now the Czech Republic), and most of Italy.

The war was hard for the German states. Farms were destroyed and businesses and cities were left in ruins. The population of the German states dropped 30 percent. About 8 million of Germany's 21 million people were killed.

The Thirty Years' War caused many German people to yearn for a place that was free of war. They wanted to live where they could practice their religions as they pleased, without being threatened. They had heard of such a place across the Atlantic Ocean. This place promised religious freedom and a new start in life. It was called America, and it began to pull many Germans to its shores. ✦

Opposite: *William Penn, an English Quaker, is shown signing a treaty with American Indian leaders that would allow German immigrants to settle on Indian land in Pennsylvania.*

# Chapter One

# The First German Settlement

*Pennsylvania, 1683–1700*

# From Penn to Pastorius

Although some Germans arrived in America earlier, most historians agree that the year 1683 marked the beginning of major German immigration. In that year, 13 families from the town of Krefeld (in the northwestern area of modern-day Germany) arrived in America. Historians often refer to these immigrants as the Krefelders, after their hometown. Sometimes the Krefelders are called the "original 13." Their new life began with an invitation from an Englishman named William Penn.

Penn, born in 1644, followed the Quaker faith, also called the Religious Society of Friends. Quakers believe in living simply, and they do not believe in violence for any reason, including war. Penn often wrote and spoke about religious freedom. He was jailed numerous times in Great Britain for his writings about religion.

Penn's father was Admiral William Penn. The British government owed money to Admiral Penn. To pay the older Penn back, the government gave the younger Penn some land in Britain's North American colonies across the Atlantic Ocean. This land is known today as Pennsylvania.

Penn decided to use his new land for what he called a "Holy Experiment." In a published brochure, he promised settlers that they could freely practice religion however they chose. This brochure was translated into German. Eventually it landed in the hands of a German named Francis Daniel Pastorius.

Pastorius was unhappy with Germany and Europe. He had been educated as a lawyer, but he decided that practicing law was not for him. While traveling across Europe, he also felt that the young Germans he met were too vain and that they did not take religion seriously. Penn's invitation to move to a country of inexpensive land and religious tolerance appealed to him.

Pastorius set sail for the new land. He purchased 15,000 acres (6,000 ha) from Penn in order to establish a new community. The land he purchased was very rugged and full of woods. Pastorius described the land as "Es ist alles nur Wald." Translated into English, this means, "All is forest." Pastorius set up his home in a cave to await the arrival of other immigrants from Germany.

# The Original 13 Arrive

In the summer of 1683, 13 families from the German town of Krefeld stood on the banks of the Rhine River. They were waiting for a boat to transport them to Rotterdam, a city in the Netherlands. The families were about to start a new life outside of Germany. Their new life would begin thousands of miles away in a new land that many people knew little about. And once they left Germany, they were not likely to return.

In all, 34 people boarded the boat on the Rhine that day. After arriving in Rotterdam, the families crossed the English Channel (a strip of water that separates Great Britain from mainland Europe) and arrived in London, England. Finally they set sail for America aboard the ship *Concord* on July 24, 1683. More than two months later, the *Concord* arrived in Philadelphia, Pennsylvania. The date was October 6, 1683.

Pastorius had arrived three months ahead of the Krefelders. In that time, he had planned out a new town of about 5,700 acres (2,300 ha) in an area just north of Philadelphia. He named it Germantown. Each family was granted three acres (1.2 ha) on which to build a home. Before the homes were built, the families lived in caves, just as Pastorius had been doing.

Pastorius and the Krefelders decided to build their homes along a trail often used by Native Americans. This trail was at first named the Great Road, then was known as Germantown Road and Main Street. Eventually it was named Germantown Avenue.

The first homes built along Germantown Avenue were log cabins and houses made of sod. (Sod is the upper layer of soil bound together by grass.) The settlers' log cabins were modeled after homes they had built in Germany. Logs were laid horizontally. Mud was then placed in between the logs to keep out the wind, dirt, rain, and snow. This style of building would soon become

*The home of Francis Daniel Pastorius, a German immigrant, was one of the largest houses in Germantown.*

popular across America as many other settlers followed the Germans' simple design. Once homes had been built, the next step in setting up a new community was creating businesses.

## The Rittenhouses

William Rittenhouse was a German who made paper. In Germany, his name was Wilhelm Rittenhaus. As with many immigrants, his name was changed so it was easier for English people to read and understand. Rittenhouse arrived in America a few years after the Krefelders. In 1690, he built the first paper mill in America. For the next few decades, the paper made at his mill in Germantown was the only American-made paper used for printing in the cities of Philadelphia and New York.

One of William's descendants was named David. David Rittenhouse became a well-known clockmaker, writer, and astronomer. Rittenhouse Square in Philadelphia was named after him.

# Work in a New Country

The Germantown settlers included a mix of craftspeople and farmers. Farmers grew crops and tended livestock to provide food for the new community. The craftspeople were skilled at making the things the new settlers needed. The craftspeople included tanners who made animal hides into leather for shoes, saddles, and harnesses. Blacksmiths worked with metal to make horseshoes, nails, and tools. The craftspeople sold or traded with each other or farmers to support their families.

Some of the first German immigrants were skilled farmers. They brought new ways of farming such as crop rotation to

America. By planting crops in different fields each year and planting different crops together, they preserved the nutrients in the soil. This made their farms very productive. German farming methods soon spread to other parts of America.

One of the first new businesses to be built in Germantown was a gristmill. A gristmill grinds wheat and other seeds into flour. The flour is then used to make bread and other baked goods. Farmers brought their grain to the mill and often paid the miller by giving him a portion of the flour, which he traded or sold to other farmers or craftspeople.

In addition to making and growing the things they needed. The new settlers hunted animals in the forests. The forests surrounding Germantown were filled with deer, wild turkeys, and other animals they hunted for food. The immigrants also traded with the Lenni Lenape (formerly called the Delaware) who were skilled hunters. The Indians especially liked the metal and leather goods made by the new settlers.

## Linen

One of the major industries of Germantown was the production of linen. Linen is a fabric made from the flax plant. Many of the German immigrants were linen weavers, and soon they were selling their linens in Philadelphia. Linen was such an important industry in the town that the town seal, designed by Daniel Pastorius, showed a flax flower.

*The Quaker religion grew with the arrival of German immigrants.*
*In the 1600s German Quakers in Pennsylvania held meetings to discuss*
*issues of the day, most important their strong stance against slavery.*

# Religion and Slavery

Many people who immigrated to the colonies were seeking the freedom to practice their religions however they chose. Many Germans who arrived in Germantown chose to join the Quaker faith. This was the religion practiced by William Penn.

The Quakers were strongly against violence. That also meant that they were against slavery. The German Quakers of Germantown wrote what is believed to be the first document ever to protest slavery. It was written in 1688, supposedly at a meeting at the home of Thones Kunders, one of the original Krefelders. Pastorius was also at this meeting. Today, a plaque stands on the site where the document is believed to have been signed, at the corner of Germantown Avenue and Wister Street. The plaque declares: "First Protest Against Slavery."

## Before There Were Settlers

Before Europeans settled the lands of Pennsylvania, the area was occupied by Native Americans. According to Daniel Pastorius, the Lenni Lenape "have accepted a sum of money from William Penn and have withdrawn very far away from us, into the wild forest, where they support themselves by the chase, shooting birds and game, and also by catching fish. They exchange their elk and deer-skins, beaver, martin [a type of bird], and turkeys for powder, lead, blankets, and brandy."

Another Protestant religious group that settled in Germantown was the Mennonites. This group originated in Switzerland and the Netherlands. Many Mennonites also came from southern Germany. Jakob Amman was a Swiss Mennonite who established the Amish religion. In the 1700s, the Amish settled west of Germantown. They became known as the Pennsylvania Dutch.

Germantown, along with the German immigrant population in America, was growing. From its original 13 families in 1683, Germantown had grown to 64 families by 1700. As the American colonies moved into the next century, German immigrants would continue to arrive. By 1790, over 500 families—about 3,000 people—were living in Germantown. 

Opposite: *A woodcut of William Penn meeting the Lenni Lenape Indians illustrates how his Quaker ideals led to a peaceful and cooperative relationship with the Native Americans living in and around his colony.*

# Chapter Two

# Overcoming Obstacles

*The Journey to America*

*When German immigrants journeyed to America, they brought all their possessions with them. These immigrants from the 1600s are landing in America for the first time with their farm animals, clothes, and farming equipment.*

# A Three-Part Journey

The arrival of the Krefelders in 1683 was just the start of German immigration to the colonies. As the years passed, more and more Germans decided to emigrate to the colonies. Many Germans who had found success in America wrote home to friends and relatives. In their letters, they praised this new land and all its opportunities. They were free to practice their own religions. They were free to pursue their own crafts and businesses.

There was enough land for everyone who could afford it, and the soil was rich for planting. Many German immigrants loved their new homeland, and they invited others to join them.

The life that awaited the new immigrants in America seemed much better than what they left behind. But the journey from Germany to the colonies was long and difficult. Most Germans took the same route, similar to the route the Krefelders had taken—down the Rhine River to Rotterdam, across the English Channel to England, and across the Atlantic Ocean to America

Each step of the journey was filled with hardships. The Rhine River had 26 customhouses, similar to modern-day tollbooths. Stopping and waiting at each customhouse made the journey very long. A German named Gottlieb Mittelberger described this part of the trip in his book *Journey to Pennsylvania in the year 1750:*

> *This journey lasts from the beginning of May to the end of October, fully half a year, amid such hardships as no one is able to describe adequately with their misery. The cause is because the Rhine's boats from Heilbronn to Holland [the Netherlands] have to pass by 26 custom houses, at all of which the ships are examined, which is done when it suits the convenience of the custom-house officials. In the meantime the ships with the people are detained long, so that the passengers have to spend much money. The trip down the Rhine lasts therefore four, five and even six weeks.*

When the immigrants finally reached Rotterdam, they were delayed again: "When the ships come to Holland, they are detained there likewise five to six weeks. Because things are very dear [expensive] there, the poor people have to spend nearly all they have during that time." In Rotterdam (or occasionally Amsterdam), the immigrants boarded another boat. This boat crossed the English Channel and docked in an English port. There, the German immigrants had another one- to two-week stay while they waited for a ship that was going to the colonies.

The journey from England to America took a little over two months. As Mittelberger explained, "[T]he real misery begins with the long voyage. For from there the ships, unless they have a good wind, must often sail eight, nine, ten to twelve weeks before they reach Philadelphia. But even with the best wind the voyage lasts seven weeks."

The length of the ocean journey added to the hardships the passengers had to endure. The passengers were all crowded together, often without enough food or water. Because of the crowded conditions and the lack of proper nutrition, many people became ill. According to Mittelberger, when he made the crossing, 32 children died. Mittelberger also describes what happened aboard ship when the seas turned rough:

> *The misery reaches the climax when a gale rages for two or three nights and days, so that every one believes that the ship will go to the bottom with all human beings on board. . . . When in such a gale the sea rages and surges, so that the waves rise often like mountains one above the other, and often tumble over the ship, so that one fears to go down with the ship; when the ship is constantly tossed from side to side by the storm and waves, so that no one can either walk or sit, or lie, and the closely packed people in the berths are thereby tumbled over each other, both the sick and the well—it will be readily understood that many of these people, none of whom had been prepared for hardships, suffer so terribly from them that they do not survive.*

Finally, the ship sailed into Philadelphia. Even there, the immigrants experienced yet another delay. The passengers were inspected by a doctor to make sure they did not have any diseases. If passengers did have a contagious disease (one that could be passed to other people), the ship, with everyone still aboard, had to move one mile outside Philadelphia. Once the sick had been cured, the passengers were allowed to leave the ship and start their lives in their new homeland.

Even though the journey was very difficult, thousands of German immigrants completed it. The years during which the most German immigrants arrived in Philadelphia were 1749 to 1754. According to the Philadelphia passenger lists for each ship, about 37,000 Germans sailed into the port city during those years.

## Paying for Passage

Not all Germans who came to the colonies were able to afford the trip, or passage. To pay for the journey, many immigrants boarded the ships under the redemption system. These passengers promised that once they arrived in Philadelphia, they would work to pay for their passage. At the port, people who needed workers would board the newly arrived ships. They would select an immigrant and then pay the ship's captain for the immigrant's trip. The immigrant would then work for that person long enough to pay back the price of the passage. Not only did the redemption system help people get to the colonies, but many immigrants also received training and new skills in this way.

# Growing Population

In 1709 French armies were constantly raiding German towns in the Palatinate region along the Main, Neckar, and Rhine Rivers. Thousands of Germans left their homes. In order to make the journey to America, the refugees had to take ships from London. London soon became crowded with Germans who wanted to go to the colonies. Not all the Germans who arrived in London made it to the colonies, however.

The ruler of England in 1709 was Queen Anne. Because of the large numbers of Germans arriving in London, she decided that she would choose where the Germans would go. England ruled many colonies at that time, including some of those in North America, so the queen had the power to decide who could live there. She sent one group of Germans to Ireland. A few hundred others were allowed to settle in the colony of North Carolina. Nearly 3,000 Germans were allowed passage to the New York colony.

*As more German immigrants arrived in Pennsylvania, new towns such as Bethlehem, shown here, developed and prospered.*

Although some German immigrants entered the colonies at other ports along the east coast of America, Philadelphia was still the main port for immigrants at the time. Many English settlers became uneasy at such large numbers of Germans arriving in Pennsylvania. The settlers feared that the Germans would not be loyal to England. Starting in 1727, German immigrants had to swear an oath of allegiance to their new country. This meant that they had to swear that they would be loyal to their new country and never turn against it. In part, the oath said: "We . . . Late Inhabitants of the Palatinate upon the Rhine, . . . Do Solemnly promise . . . that WE will be faithful . . . to his . . . MAJESTY KING GEORGE THE SECOND and his Successors [other kings or queens who came after George II]." The oath also asked the German immigrants to promise that they would "observe [and] conform to the Laws of England and of this Province [Pennsylvania]."

# Beyond Pennsylvania

It was not long before German immigrants began to look for land beyond Pennsylvania. As more Germans arrived, the area around Philadelphia and Germantown was quickly being settled. Land for new farms and homes became scarce. Pennsylvania was not the only colony, though, and soon German immigrants were moving both north and south.

North of Pennsylvania, some German immigrants settled in New Jersey, along the Raritan River. Some immigrants traveled as far north as Maine. The more northern colonies, however, such as Massachusetts, were not as easy to settle into as Pennsylvania. Settlers had been living in Massachusetts for much longer than they had been in Pennsylvania, so not much land was available. In addition, the Puritan religion was widely practiced throughout the colonies of the Northeast. Puritans did not welcome people who practiced a religion other than theirs. Most German immigrants were not welcome.

Something very different prevented many Germans from settling in the southern colonies. This was slavery. Many Germans did not believe that owning slaves was right. Even so, some German immigrants arrived in South Carolina's port city, Charles Town (later Charleston). Most German immigrants chose not to live in the port city. Instead, they spread out to the rural, or country, areas beyond. There, they set up farms and homes. Many Germans also traveled from western Pennsylvania into the lands of Virginia.

Many German settlers went to Louisiana. In 1717, John Law published a pamphlet urging Germans to settle in the Louisiana territory. (Louisiana belonged to France at this time. It became part of the United States in 1803.) Encouraged by the pamphlet, many Germans settled there.

The one colony that many Germans were hesitant to enter was Maryland. Just as Pennsylvania had been held by William Penn, Maryland was held by a man named Lord Baltimore. Unlike the Quaker Penn, who believed in religious tolerance, Lord Baltimore was Catholic. The German settlers felt that they would not be welcome in Maryland.

Lord Baltimore convinced them that they were welcome. He invited German families to settle in the western part of the colony. He offered each family 200 acres (80 ha) of land for free for the first three years. After that time, the families would pay to rent the land from him. Soon, Germans were prospering in Maryland as well.

The number of Germans immigrating to America slowed between the years 1756 and 1763. This period marked the Seven Years' War, also called the French and Indian War. During this time, Great Britain controlled travel across the Atlantic Ocean.

Not many ships were allowed to sail, so immigrants were often stranded in Engand, unable to continue their journey to America.

## Jonathan Hager

One of the Germans who settled in Maryland was a man named Jonathan Hager. He became involved in the politics of the colonies, and he was elected to Maryland's General Assembly in 1771. At that time, there was a law that made it illegal for citizens not born in the colonies to hold a public office. Hager was told that he would not be able to accept the position in the General Assembly. The voters of Maryland were angry about this decision. After all, they had elected him. As a result, the law was reconsidered and overturned. Hager was able to take his position after the next election. The town of Hagerstown, Maryland, was founded by Jonathan Hager in 1762.

# Proving Their Loyalty

For most Germans who settled in the colonies, life was good. Even so, many did not wish to get politically involved in their new homeland. But something was soon to happen that would change their attitude and inspire German immigrants to prove their loyalty. It was the American Revolution.

The American Revolution was fought between the colonies and their ruling country of England. People in the colonies were tired of paying taxes and having to obey laws forced on them by a country across the ocean. They did not have any say about the making of these laws. The colonists felt that they could govern their own country without interference from England.

*German immigrants built forts in Pennsylvania and Ohio that would
help the Patriots during the Revolutionary War.*

Most German colonists shared this view, supporting the
idea that the colonies should break away from England. The
colonists knew that to achieve their goal they might have to go
to war with England. Although some were against war because
of their religion, they still supported the cause by providing
supplies. Some even made guns for the soldiers to use.

One German in particular was of great help to the colonists.
His name was Baron Friedrich Wilhelm Augustin von Steuben.
He was born in Prussia, a kingdom in what would later become
Germany, in 1730, and he became a soldier well known
throughout Europe. When he left the Prussian army, he began
looking for work in the army of another country. Steuben
arrived in the United States in 1777. In 1778, he joined George
Washington, the commander of the American troops, and began

training soldiers at Valley Forge, Pennsylvania. Many historians believe that his training helped the colonists become more than just fighters. They became a unified and efficient army of soldiers. Steuben became a citizen of the United States in 1784 and lived in New York.

*German-born Baron Friedrich Wilhelm Augustin von Steuben brought his outstanding skills as a soldier from Europe to help General George Washington train soldiers and organize the colonial militia.*

Although Baron von Steuben was a great help to the colonists, one group of German soldiers fought against them. They were the Hessian soldiers. These soldiers were ordered by their German states to fight with the British. Because many of the soldiers came from the German state of Hesse-Cassel, they were called Hessians. About 30,000 soldiers from Germany fought along with the British against the colonists.

Many Hessian soldiers changed their mind about fighting with the British once they arrived in America. At the time of the Revolutionary War, about 200,000 Germans were living in the colonies. Seeing these prosperous communities of Germans, many Hessians deserted their armies and fought with the colonists. Hessian soldiers that were captured in battle were often treated well by colonists. After the war, between 5,000 and 6,000 Hessian soldiers decided to remain in America.

The Revolutionary War ended in 1783. German immigrants were the largest group of non-English immigrants in the new country. And now, with the end of the war, they were no longer only Germans, or people of German descent. They were Americans.

*Opposite: A 19th-century German immigrant farmer and his horse plow a field in South Dakota. He was one of many German immigrants who settled in the Midwest and established farms in spite of the harsh weather and difficult farming conditions in that part of the United States.*

# Chapter Three

# New Country, New Challenges

## *The Mid-19th Century*

# European Unrest

With the end of the Revolutionary War in 1783, the individual colonies became a unified country called the United States of America. The people who had come from Europe to this new country had a new identity. They may have come from England or France or Ireland or Germany, but they were now all Americans. And with the birth of this new nation, its citizens had new challenges to face.

The years following the Revolutionary War were slow ones for German immigration. Not as many Germans were immigrating to the United States as before the war. Bad times in Europe were the biggest reason for this slowdown.

When the Thirty Years' War had ended in 1648, many of the German states were in ruins. Poor people were left with very little. Many fled from their homes. Their land was soon taken over by the upper classes, or the nobility, of the German states. Because the poor Germans suffered and wanted to leave, wealthier Germans prospered by getting more land. In addition, many of the rulers of the German states continued to gain power.

# The Fall of Prussia

One of the German states at this time was Prussia. Prussia's leader, Friedrich Wilhelm, and later his sons, expanded its territory. In the late 1700s, Prussia was one of the most powerful regions in Europe.

Then, in 1789, the French Revolution broke out. This war was fought between the lower classes and the nobility of France. The lower classes were fighting for better living conditions, and their goal was to overthrow the monarchy. A man who gained significant power during this time was Napoleon Bonaparte. He gained prominence and recognition while fighting and commanding the French army in Italy. Bonaparte eventually overthrew the monarchy himself, and he proclaimed himself the emperor of France.

At first, countries throughout Europe embraced the new French government and its emperor. Many European leaders supported a more democratic France. They felt that this form of government was much better than one controlled by a monarch. The countries that had a supreme ruler themselves, however, opposed the new government of France. They saw it as a threat to their way of governing. The German state of Prussia was one of those opposing states, as was the state of Austria.

*A painting by the German artist F. Dietz shows peasants after the French army invaded the town of Leipzig, Germany. Napoleon's campaign to conquer Europe, including Germany, caused many Germans to flee to America.*

Napoleon was not the democratic leader that people had hoped for. He began a series of campaigns across Europe to take over more lands for France. Once again, Germany was under attack. On July 12, 1806, Napoleon set up the Confederation of the Rhine. This area included all the German states except Prussia, Austria, Brunswick, and Hessen. Now most of Germany was controlled by Napoleon. On October

*Napoleon Bonaparte, the emperor of France, directs his troops in battle from horseback.*

14, 1806, Napoleon beat the Prussian army and took over Berlin. Prussia was reduced to nearly half its size. Seven years later, in 1813, Prussia tried to conquer Napoleon but failed.

Napoleon's reign could not last forever. A few months after Prussia's failed attempt to conquer him, Napoleon and his troops were pushed back across the Rhine River. In 1814, the Prussians, along with the Austrians and the Russians, attacked France. Riding into Paris in March of that year, they forced Napoleon to leave France and live in exile on an island in the Mediterranean Sea.

Napoleon would not give up, however, and he once again raised an army and battled Great Britain, Prussia, Austria, and

Russia. Eventually he was defeated in 1815 at the Battle of Waterloo. This time he was permanently exiled to St. Helena, an island in the southern Atlantic Ocean far off the coast of Africa.

With Napoleon now out of the picture, the four main powers of Europe (Prussia, Austria, Great Britain, and Russia) set about trying to restore order. One thing they sought was the unification of all the states of Germany into one country. Although this idea met with some approval, diplomats from Prussia and Austria were against it. A compromise was reached, and the German Confederation was established. It united 39 German states, not including Prussia and Austria. Austria was granted the right to oversee the new confederation. Prussia was granted lands in other German states.

# Conflict in America

While the German states and the rest of Europe were battling Napoleon, the United States had its own conflict, called the War of 1812.

In a sense, Napoleon was involved with this war, too. His armies were fighting Great Britain in Europe. Great Britain felt that it had the right to seize any ships on the ocean, especially those that sailed to or from a port in Napoleon's empire. In addition, British sea captains would board American ships and impress, or force, American sailors into English service. The United States tried to remain neutral about the conflicts in Europe, but the seizure of its ships and sailors made neutrality impossible. War ensued, and it lasted until 1815.

With the wars in Europe and in the United States finally over, Germans once again began venturing to America in search of a new homeland.

*Here a poor family receives food from a rich woman during the 1800s.
Many Germans who were reduced to poverty as a result of the
Napoleonic Wars fled to America, seeking a better life.*

# Come to Missouri!

Many Germans who had arrived in America in the late 18th century had left Germany in search of religious freedom. In the 1800s, many Germans were now seeking better living conditions. Some Germans simply moved within Germany or Europe. After all, America had also seen several wars, and perhaps chances for a better life there were not as great as everyone believed. In the 1820s, only a handful of Germans, 6,000 to 8,000, came to America.

But living conditions for families in Germany continued to decline. After the Napoleonic Wars, items manufactured in factories in Great Britain began to arrive in Germany. People began buying these cheaper products, which put many German craftspeople out of work. In addition, land became scarce. Families could not survive on the small pieces of land that were being divided among family members. Families no longer could depend on their land for food. And they no longer could count on people to buy their crafts. These economic factors began pushing many Germans out of the country.

In 1829, a German American named Gottfried Duden wrote a book called *A Journey to the Western States of North America.* In his book, Duden described his wonderful new life on his farm in Missouri, which had become a state in 1821. "There is still room for millions of farms along the Missouri [River]," Duden claimed in his book. For many Germans, Duden's descriptions made Missouri sound like an ideal place to be.

Duden's book was not the only thing that enticed Germans to immigrate to America. Several German societies were started in the hopes of forming German communities in the new country. One such society was the Giessen Emigration Society. It was established in 1833. The society passed out pamphlets to people in Germany, encouraging them to emigrate to America. The society did not last, but it did pull many Germans to the United States.

**German Immigration to America**

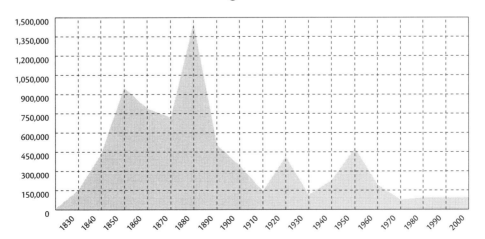

## The German State of Texas?

Some people reasoned that the Giessen Emigration Society failed because the society had tried to establish a German state within an American state. They wondered if they could successfully establish a German state in a place that was not yet part of the United States. Texas seemed like just such a place.

The program to develop a German state in Texas was called *Adelsverein*, which means "nobles club." For about $120, Germans could gain passage to Texas, along with 40 acres (16 ha) of land in west-central Texas. From 1844 to 1847, more than 7,000 Germans accepted the proposal. In 1845, however, the United States and Mexico were at war over Texas. A true German state in Texas was not to be. Even so, German settlers there wrote to people back in Germany about this wonderful land. Over the next 10 to 20 years, about 30,000 Germans emigrated to Texas.

Not all Germans who made the journey to the United States were happy with their new life. The writings by Duden and the Giessen society promised a rich, rewarding life in the United States. These writings did not mention anything about clearing land and working hard to plant and harvest and hunt. Many immigrants were disappointed by what they found in their new homeland. It was nothing like what they had expected. Some immigrants missed Europe and returned. Those who did stay worked hard to make a prosperous life.

# Rough Road Ahead

The trip to Missouri was not easy. The travelers had to endure the same foul conditions aboard ships as their predecessors had in the previous century. This time, however, the trip took much longer. Missouri is inland, about 1,000 miles (1,600 km) away from the eastern port cities of the United States. Immigrants who landed in Baltimore and Philadelphia had to then travel another 1,000 miles inland before they reached Missouri.

By the 1840s, Germans began taking another route to the Midwest. Instead of sailing to ports in the east, they sailed to the southern port of New Orleans, Louisiana. There, they boarded steamboats, which traveled up the Mississippi River. But even this trip could take several weeks, and it was sometimes dangerous. In 1852 alone, 67 steamboat accidents occurred on rivers in the west, and 466 people lost their lives.

# City Life

When German immigrants first began to arrive in America, most of them had settled in rural areas to set up farms. This practice continued in the 1800s. In fact, many German immigrants in Missouri were called "Latin farmers" because of the formal, classical education they had received in Europe.

In the 1800s, more German immigrants began settling in cities. Craftspeople often found it easier to practice their craft in the city rather than buy land and learn how to farm it. Some people worked in the city in order to earn enough money to buy land. Others were content to remain in the city. Cities also offered jobs for workers with little or no skills or experience.

## It's a Fact!

The first German-language newspaper in America was published in Pennsylvania in 1732. It was called the *Philadelphische Zeitung.* (*Zeitung* is German for "newspaper.")
A little more than 100 years later, in 1836, a German-language newspaper was published in St. Louis. It was called *Anzeiger des Westens,* which means "Report of the West." By 1860, about 200 German-language newspapers were being published in the United States.

## Friedrich Froebel

*Kindergarten* is a German word. The first part of the word, *Kinder*, means "children." The second part of the word, *garten*, means "garden." Translated literally, a *kindergarten* is a garden of children. Friedrich Froebel created this word himself. He felt it expressed his ideas about early childhood education. A Web site dedicated to Froebel's ideas explains: "Children are like tiny flowers; they are varied and need care, but each is beautiful alone and glorious when seen in the community of peers." In 1852, the word *kindergarten* appeared in a dictionary for the first time.

One city that saw an explosion of German immigrants was St. Louis, Missouri. St. Louis sits at the juncture of the Mississippi and Missouri Rivers. Many travelers passed through St. Louis on their way to other places. Some of the travelers decided to stay. In 1833, only 18 German families lived in St. Louis. Four years later, that number had mushroomed to about 6,000 people.

German immigrants helped establish St. Louis as a thriving city. Craftspeople, such as carpenters, tailors, blacksmiths, and bakers, provided much-needed services. Germans also set up restaurants, stores, and boarding houses (places where people rented rooms). In 1850, the population of St. Louis was 78,000. Nearly a third of that population was German. Their political ideas would influence state policy in Missouri in the years to come.

# The Forty-Eighters

Europe in the mid-1800s was still a land of instability. The German states especially were not very stable. Even though the German Confederation had been established earlier in the century, each German state was still led by its own ruler rather than a democratic government. Many people in Germany wanted a government that allowed all people to participate, not just the wealthy. In 1848, uprisings and revolts broke out across Germany, and throughout Europe, in an attempt to squash the rulers. When the uprisings failed, several thousand people fled Germany to find refuge and safety in the United States. They were afraid of being severely punished or even killed for their revolt against the German rulers. The people who came to the United States from Germany at this time became known as the "Forty-Eighters."

The Forty-Eighters had been active in politics in Germany, and they continued to be active in American politics as well. Carl Schurz was one of the Forty-Eighters. Schurz settled in Missouri after the German revolts of 1848. He became a well-respected journalist and politician. He campaigned for the Republican political party during the election of 1860. With Schurz's help, Abraham Lincoln was elected president of the United States.

America itself was about to erupt into war, and many German Americans would prove themselves on the battlefield.

> ## It's a Fact!
>
> **Carl Schurz served as U.S. envoy to Spain under President Lincoln and was elected to the Senate in 1869. President Rutherford Hayes appointed Schurz to the post of secretary of the interior, where he pushed for the development of national parks. Schurz also fought for civil service reforms for Native Americans.**

# Kindergarten Comes to America

Margarethe Meyer Schurz was Carl Schurz's wife. She left Germany with her husband in 1848. In 1856, she started the first kindergarten in the United States in Watertown, Wisconsin. In Germany, a man named Friedrich Froebel had started the first kindergarten in 1837. He believed that games, songs, stories, and crafts could help young children develop both mentally and physically. This would help them learn better later on. Froebel's ideas about kindergarten slowly spread across Germany and even into England.

Margarethe Schurz agreed with Froebel's ideas. At first, she cared for and educated her own daughter and four neighborhood children. She read them stories, and the children sang songs, played games, and created art projects.

Then Schurz began a small kindergarten class, open to all children. Soon, kindergarten classes began to spring up around the country. By 1883, every public school in St. Louis, Missouri, had a kindergarten. By 1920, nearly every public school in the United States had a kindergarten class.

*This 19th-century illustration shows a typical kindergarten class.*

# The Civil War

Many Germans had fled Europe to escape a country plagued by wars. In 1860, war came to America when the Southern states decided to secede from the United States (called "the Union"). *Secede* means to withdraw or remove oneself from an organized body. With the secession of the Southern states, the U.S. Civil War (1861–1865) became a horrible reality.

Many German Americans had mixed feelings about the war. As with the Revolutionary War, some were opposed to the war because of their religion. Many German Americans also opposed slavery, so they favored the politics of the Northern states, where slavery had been outlawed. A large number of German Americans also felt that the very act of seceding from the Union was wrong. The Southern states' decision reminded them of revolts in Europe. These German Americans supported their new country, and they did not agree with the states that wanted to secede.

During the course of the war, thousands of German Americans fought for the Union. Many thousands died or were injured. One of the German Americans' most important contributions to the war occurred in Missouri.

Technically, Missouri was a slave state. Slavery was legal there. Even so, farmers did not depend much on slaves, and slavery was never widely accepted. Still, the Confederacy (those states that had seceded) wanted Missouri to secede from the Union also.

In an effort to make sure that Missouri stayed on the side of the Confederacy, Confederate soldiers called Minute Men attempted to take over Missouri. However, Union troops stopped and captured the Minute Men at Camp Jackson. Many of these Union troops were German volunteers. Historians believe that the success of the Union army at Camp Jackson prevented Missouri from siding with the Confederacy and seceding from the Union.

Along with supporting their own ideals, many German Americans also participated in the war for another reason. They wished to prove to the United States that they were loyal and dedicated to their new homeland. Fighting in the Civil War proved that the Germans were not just immigrants, but Americans willing to fight for their new country.

Throughout the mid-1800s, German immigration rose steadily. In the 1830s, nearly 125,000 Germans emigrated to the United States. In the 1840s, that number more than tripled to 385,000. And during the 1850s, the number of German immigrants was close to 1 million. The 1860s saw a slight decline in immigrants, probably because of the Civil War. Even so, by 1860, about 1.3 million German-born immigrants lived in the United States. The record number of immigrants in the 1850s would be shattered in the next few decades. 

Opposite: *German immigrant Henry J. Heinz started selling pickles from carts like this one in Pittsburg, Pennsylvania, in the 1860s. Later he added sauces, including ketchup, to his carts. Heinz pioneered the use of slogans such as "Heinz 57 Varieties," and his was one of the first companies to use advertising to sell its products.*

*Chapter Four*

# Moving Westward and Upward

*German Americans Prosper*

# The Unsettled West

The greatest wave of German immigration to the United States was about to begin. But the United States was not the young nation it had once been. Land was becoming harder to get because much of the country had been settled. Jobs in overcrowded cities were becoming harder to find. The skills of craftspeople were no longer needed because many items were made in factories. Still, German immigrants began to arrive in record numbers.

In 1862, the United States passed a new law. It was called the Homestead Act. It allowed people to settle 160 acres (64 ha) of government-owned land, almost for free. This land was in all parts of the United States, except for the thirteen original colonies and the states of Maine, Vermont, West Virginia,

*The Homestead Act of 1862 was commemorated in 1962 on a U.S. postage stamp.*

Kentucky, Tennessee, and Texas. Most of the available lands, therefore, were in the unsettled West.

The Homestead Act stated that anyone who was 21 years old, or the head of a household, could claim the 160 acres. The settler then had to live on the land for five years, build a home, and plant crops. After those five years, if it had been proved that he or she could care for it, the settler would own the land. The only money required was an $18 filing fee.

One of the things that made this act so special was that nearly anyone could file for a land claim. It did not matter if a person's family had lived in the United States for 100 years or 100 days. It did not matter if a person was born in the United States or had just arrived. Generally, in the past, only white men could own land. The Homestead Act let everyone, including women and former slaves, claim 160 acres.

The population of the United States was growing, and land in the east was becoming scarce. The Homestead Act not only encouraged people to move west, it also ensured that these vast western lands would be settled. The land had been occupied by American Indian tribes, but these tribes were pushed off the land and onto reservations in order to encourage white settlement and the westward expansion of the United States. While this was extremely unfair to the Indians, it was a good opportunity for immigrants and others who wanted to own land.

Some German immigrants traveled farther than the Midwest. Like many Americans, German immigrants were lured by the prospect of finding gold in California in the mid-1800s. Yet most German immigrants continued to settle in the Midwest.

*This thatched stable was typical of farm buildings built by German immigrants in the 1800s. It has been preserved and restored in Eagle, Wisconsin.*

# The Russian Germans of the 1870s

I n the mid-1700s, Germans had immigrated not only to the United States, but to Russia as well. The czars (rulers) of Russia at that time, Catherine the Great (1729–1796) and then Alexander I (1777–1825), had encouraged German farmers to settle in an undesirable part of Russia called the Russian steppes. This area was mostly dry grassland that had not yet been developed. Many Germans, accepting their invitation, began setting up communities along the Volga River and the Black Sea.

As the decades passed, about 300 colonies of German settlers were established in Russia. These German settlers did not associate much with their Russian neighbors. Instead, they remained within their communities, farmed their lands, attended their own churches, and kept their own language and culture.

In 1870, the Russian government decided that the Germans were no longer welcome in Russia. The lands the Germans had cultivated for decades were taken away from them. But instead of returning to Germany, many Russian Germans decided to head to the United States. The lure of the land was enough to pull these immigrants thousands of miles away.

Because the Russian Germans had experience with cultivating dry grasslands, many chose to move to the Great Plains of North America. Some of these German immigrants settled in the plains of Canada. Others moved to the plains of North and South Dakota, Nebraska, Colorado, and Kansas.

Many historians credit this group of German immigrants with transforming the Great Plains into a highly productive farming area. In Russia, the Russian Germans had started growing a type of wheat called red hard winter wheat. This wheat came from Turkey, and it grew very well in Russia. The Russian Germans who immigrated to the United States brought some of these wheat seeds with them.

Planting the wheat on the grasslands of the Great Plains proved to be just as successful as it was in Russia. This ability to grow wheat helped the United States to become more self-sufficient. The country could now produce its own wheat and did not have to import it from other countries. This was a very important achievement for the United States.

*Russian-German farmers were successful growing red hard winter wheat in North Dakota and other plains states. Farmers use a mechanical harvester in this photo from about 1900.*

## Russian Germans, the Railroads, and Kansas

A large community of Russian Germans settled in Kansas. According to the Kansas State Historical Society, about 12,000 Russian Germans lived in Kansas by 1879. Many Russian Germans were lured to Kansas by railroad companies. At that time, two major railroad companies, the Kansas Pacific and the Atchison, Topeka & Santa Fe, owned much of the land along their railroad lines. They wished to settle these lands with wheat farmers, then ship the wheat using their railroads. The railroad companies sent people to Russia to convince the Russian Germans to come to Kansas.

On September 10, 1874, the *Topeka Commonwealth* newspaper described these new immigrants in this way: "They were all Germans, but having lived all their lives in Russia, their German [language] has a curious Russian flavor." The Russian Germans settled into communities similar to the ones they left behind. They did not mix much with American culture, preferring to stay mostly with people of their own background.

# A Unified Germany

The political situation was changing not only in Russia, but in Germany as well. Prussia had once again gained prominence, and in the 1860s it began following a new leader, Otto von Bismarck. Bismarck was Prussia's prime minister, and Wilhelm I was its king. Bismarck believed strongly in a unified Germany because he wanted Prussia to be the ultimate power in Europe. One by one, he began absorbing other German states into the Prussian government. A short war with Austria helped to solidify Prussia's dominance. Austria did not become part of the unified Germany, but instead joined with Hungary to become an empire, called Austria-Hungary, in 1867.

Only four German states had yet to join Bismarck's unified Germany. These were Bavaria, Baden, Wurttemberg, and Hesse-Darmstadt. Hoping that the four states would join German forces to fight against a common enemy, Bismarck started a war with France. His plan was a success. By fighting for Germany, those states became part of the new Germany. On January 18, 1871, the German Empire was born. For the first time, all the German states were united into one country. The king of Prussia, Wilhelm I, became the emperor of Germany.

# Boom and Bust

In the United States, the unification of Germany brought about a rise in German awareness and German pride. But the unification did not stop people in Germany from emigrating. In fact, the 1880s saw the largest number of German immigrants to the United States. During that decade, almost 1.5 million Germans left their homeland to come to America. In 1882 alone, nearly 250,000 arrived.

During past waves of immigration, most of the German immigrants had come from the northern or western German states. Most of them were Protestant. In the latter half of the 1800s, Germans from more eastern and southern states began to emigrate, as well as those from Russia.

Also in the late 1800s, Germans who followed the Roman Catholic Church began to emigrate. The new unified Germany made it clear that it wished to be a country of Protestantism. It did not want to be influenced by the Roman Catholic Church. So many Roman Catholic Germans left. Germans of the Jewish faith had also started coming to America, beginning in the 1830s. At that time, some German states passed laws against the Jewish faith. German Jews continued to emigrate for many decades.

# An Easier Crossing

Another reason for the large number of immigrants in the late 1800s was the availability of transportation by steamship and train. The journey to America was no longer as lengthy or as difficult as it once had been. People could now take trains to port cities in Europe. The trains traveled much faster than the Rhine riverboats.

Instead of taking months to sail across the ocean, steamships (ships powered by steam instead of the wind) could cross the ocean in two to three weeks. Steamships were also much more comfortable for travelers. By the 1900s, immigrants could travel from Hamburg, Germany, directly to New York City on a steamship.

Ships carrying immigrants also pulled into the port cities of Boston (Massachusetts), Philadelphia, Baltimore, Mobile (Alabama), New Orleans, Galveston (Texas), San Francisco, and Seattle (Washington). And once the immigrants landed in the United States, they could take a train to the Midwest or wherever they wanted to go. No longer did they need to travel by river, on horseback, or even on foot.

But a comfortable, prosperous life for immigrants in the United States was not as easy to come by in the late 1800s as it had been during earlier decades. The population of America was blossoming. Not only were many people from all over the world coming into the country to live, but already established families continued to grow. Cities were overcrowded, and rooms were hard to find. Large families sometimes lived in very small, cramped apartments.

When the United States was first being developed, not many craftspeople lived there. New towns needed craftspeople who had a learned skill, such as clock making. German immigrants had readily filled those positions. By the late 1800s, however, America had plenty of craftspeople. Many immigrants who lived in cities discovered that their skills were not needed. In addition, many products, such as clocks, were now made in factories. People preferred to buy these factory-made products because they did not cost as much money as those made by hand.

A skilled clock maker from Germany could probably find work in a clock factory, but the work was not satisfying. The hours were long, and the work boring and tedious. Instead of applying skill to the art of making a clock, a worker would perform a single task in the clock-making process over and over and over again, every day. It was not the life the immigrants had hoped for when they left Germany.

# Problems and Protests

Many German immigrants soon became unhappy with their life in the United States. They wanted better working and living conditions. To achieve this goal, they decided to form labor unions. Labor unions are organizations that strive to make sure that all workers in a business are treated fairly. Although people from many backgrounds joined the labor unions, the majority of members in most unions were German.

The labor unions were not popular with American businesses. Labor unions demanded higher wages, shorter working hours, as well as safer working conditions. These changes meant that businesses had to spend money to improve their factories or increase their workers' pay. The fact that many Germans were part of the labor unions aroused some anti-German sentiment in America. That means that many people did not like or approve of the German Americans living and working in their communities.

This was not the first time that German immigrants had faced prejudice from other Americans. Some Americans whose families had lived in the United States for generations considered themselves "true" Americans who were superior to more recent immigrants. These nativists were not just against German immigrants. They were opposed to all immigrants. They wanted the government to set up anti-immigration laws that would prevent further immigration or at least limit the number of immigrants who could enter the country.

# Still a Place to Prosper

Even though life was not easy for some immigrants, many German Americans did prosper during this time. German immigrant Henry J. Heinz started the Heinz food company. Its first product was his mother's recipe for horseradish, a pungent herb used in cooking. The company began making sauces in 1876, including ketchup. The Heinz business eventually became a success. Many people found work in Heinz factories.

In 1853, a German immigrant named Henry Engelhard Steinway started a company that built pianos. Although it was a small business at first, the quality of Steinway's pianos became well respected. When he died in 1871, Steinway's sons took over the business. They kept improving their piano designs, and their business flourished.

*Henry Engelhard Steinway crafted pianos using design techniques perfected by German immigrants.*

Steinway & Sons is still a thriving company. It makes about 5,000 pianos a year.

Today, the Bausch & Lomb company is well-known for making contact lenses and other eye-care products. The company started back in 1853, when a German immigrant named John Jacob Bausch started a small eyeglass shop in Rochester, New York. Bausch came up with the idea of making frames for eyeglasses from plastic. People liked these new glasses because they did not break easily. By the 1870s, the Bausch & Lomb company (Henry Lomb became Bausch's partner) had a sales office in New York City and large factory in Rochester.

# A New Era

The United States had seen many changes since the Krefelders landed in 1683. By 1890, about 2.8 million German-born immigrants lived in the United States. The number of immigrants

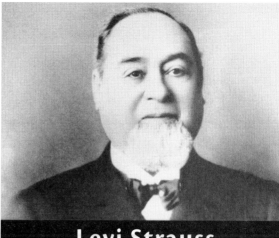

## Levi Strauss

Levi Strauss, the inventor of blue jeans, came from the German state of Bavaria. He arrived in San Francisco, California, in 1850. Although he might have hoped to find gold, his main goal was to provide supplies for the gold miners. Strauss was a tailor (a tailor sews clothes for a living). He thought that people in California would need tents and covers for their wagons, which he would sew from canvas material. But the miners did not need these items. What they needed was sturdy, durable clothing. So Strauss sewed the canvas he had brought for tents and wagon covers into pants, and the first pairs of jeans were born. Eventually, Strauss changed the material from canvas to a blue denim. He opened a factory in San Francisco, and today people still buy his blue jeans, also called "Levi's."

began to decline in the 1900s. Some figures show that in 1910, about 2.3 million German-born immigrants lived in America, and by 1920 that number had dwindled to 1.7 million as older immigrants died.

Even so, the German population in America remained strong because many Americans had German ancestors. New waves of German immigrants would soon come to the United States, although not as many as during the 1800s. 

Opposite: *In this picture, Jewish children arrive in New York City aboard the S.S.* Harding. *Many Jewish children fleeing persecution from the growing anti-Semitism in Germany in the first part of the 20th century were adopted by American families.*

# Chapter Five

# A World at War

*Trouble for Germans*

# Leading Up to War

Throughout their history in the United States, German immigrants had met very little prejudice or resistance. At times, Germans were even invited to help settle the vast lands of the United States. The twentieth century, however, would see growing anti-German feelings, especially when the United States fought two wars against Germany.

When Otto von Bismarck unified Germany in 1871, many European countries became nervous. They were concerned that Germany might become a power to be feared. If Germany decided to increase its size, the borders of such countries as France and Belgium might be threatened.

Even though the United States was an ocean away from Germany, it was also nervous about the new German empire. In 1890, the emperor of Germany was Wilhelm II. He was known as Kaiser Wilhelm. Many people believed that Kaiser Wilhelm wanted to rule the world. People in America thought that his intentions could include the United States, too. When German Americans began to form their own societies, or clubs, many other Americans worried that German Americans could be working with Kaiser Wilhelm to take over the United States. These suspicions led to negative feelings toward German Americans.

# World War I

Relationships between European countries had been tense for many years. In June 1914, the heir to the throne of the empire of Austria-Hungary was assassinated. The Austrians blamed the neighboring country of Serbia and declared war. Soon other European countries chose sides and entered the war, too.

Russia fought with Serbia, and Germany joined forces with Austria-Hungary. France then decided to fight with the Russians.

Germany had often worried what might happen if it fought a war against both France and Russia. Germany sat squarely between both countries. It could be attacked on its western border by France or on its eastern border by Russia.

Kaiser Wilhelm, Germany's leader, decided to try to defeat France first. In order to do so, he decided to first invade Belgium. Belgium had claimed to be neutral in the war, meaning that it would not take sides. The British government, on the other hand, had promised that if Belgium was attacked, Britain would defend it. When Germany invaded Belgium, Britain lived up to its promise. Britain was now involved in the war as well.

*The British luxury liner* Lusitania *left New York Harbor on May 1, 1915. The sinking of the cruise ship by a German submarine six days later contributed to the United States' decision to enter World War II.*

It became harder and harder for the United States to remain neutral. In 1917, the United States officially entered World War I. Many German Americans were torn by what was happening. Even though they had left their homeland and started new lives in the United States, they still felt some loyalty to Germany. Many German immigrants had continued to follow their German customs and traditions, and many were proud to be both German and American. They wanted to defend the actions of Germany. But at the same time, they wanted to support their new country, too. More anti-German sentiment arose in the United States.

The German Americans' plight worsened when the British intercepted a telegram on January 17, 1917. The telegram was being sent by Germany's foreign minister to Mexico, Arthur Zimmermann. It encouraged Mexico to start a war with the United States. That way, the United States would be too busy defending its own lands to fight against Germany in Europe.

The telegram was disastrous for German Americans. Many people in the United States thought that Germany wanted to start a war with America. They began to hate everything German, including German Americans.

# Against Everything German

Everything that had a German connection was suddenly considered bad in the United States. German music, including music by such classical composers as Ludwig von

Beethoven and Johann Sebastian Bach, was banned. Schools no longer taught the German language. Towns with German names changed their names. For example, Germantown, Nebraska, was changed to Garland, Nebraska. Statues of famous German people were removed from town squares.

Many German Americans tried to hide their German roots. They quickly became American citizens. Many changed their names so they sounded more American. They stopped speaking German and practicing many of their German customs and traditions.

*This 1918 poster encourages Americans to buy Liberty Bonds to help defeat the "Hun"—a negative term used to describe German soldiers during World War I.*

One of the most telling examples of German Americans hiding their background can be found in the United States census, a count taken every 10 years to determine the population of the United States. According to the census of 1910, about 2.3 million German-born immigrants claimed to live in America. It is known that more than 174,000 German immigrants entered the United States in the decade that followed. However, the 1920 census counted only 1.7 million German-born immigrants. Historians believe that many German-born immigrants lied to the 1920 census takers in order to hide their German roots.

## An Anti-German Law?

In January 1919, the United States government passed the Eighteenth Amendment to the Constitution. This amendment made it illegal to sell or purchase alcoholic products, including beer and wine. Because alcohol was prohibited (not allowed), this movement is historically called Prohibition. Although the government claimed that alcohol was being prohibited due to concern for people's health, some people thought that Prohibition was an anti-German law. Most of the well-known and successful brewers (beer makers) in America were German. With the Eighteenth Amendment, the breweries were put out of work, which greatly affected many German-American workers. The law was also seen as a slight against people's German heritage, because beer had always been an important part of German culture.

The second way that German Americans reacted to the outcry against everything German was just the opposite. Instead of shedding their German identities, some German Americans chose to cling to their German culture more fiercely, yet not openly. Before the war, some Germans had chosen to stay mostly to themselves and with other Germans in America. Now they isolated themselves even more. They withdrew from American society as much as possible, while associating only with other Germans. They surrounded themselves with only German culture.

Another casualty of anti-German feelings was German newspapers. At one time during the late 1800s, about 800 German-language newspapers were being published in the United States. By 1910, that number had dropped to 554. Over the next ten years, 330 papers would stop publication. In addition, German-language newspapers had to publish an English version so the government could see what they printed and make sure that the German people were not planning actions against the United States.

# After the War

World War I ended in 1918. Germany had not been victorious, and about 1.8 million people in Germany had been killed. The German economy suffered greatly from the war. German money was now practically worthless. With their country in ruins, Germans once again began emigrating to the United States. It is estimated that between 1919 and 1933, about 430,000 Germans left Germany for America. These numbers perhaps would have been higher, but in 1921 and again in 1924 the U.S. government passed laws that restricted European immigration.

An increasing number of Germans coming to the United States were Jewish. Although many Jews lived productive lives in Germany, anti-Jewish laws were being passed in their homeland. These laws were caused by a widespread attitude of anti-Semitism, or a historical hatred of Jews as a religious and ethnic group. As a result, German Jews faced increasing prejudice in their country.

The 1920s was a boom period in America. Most people were leading prosperous and fulfilling lives. In October 1929, however, the stock market crashed. Banks and businesses lost a lot of money; many lost all their money. These companies could no longer pay their workers, so people lost their jobs. When people lost their jobs, they had no money, so they could not buy things. Because no one was buying the products that factories and other businesses made, these businesses began losing money, so more people lost their jobs. That, in turn, meant that those people no longer had much money to spend. The era of the Great Depression had begun. It was a trying time not only for Americans, but for people around the world. Because of what was happening in America, the entire world also fell into a poor economic state that would not improve until the beginning of World War II in the late 1930s.

## The Stock Market Crash of 1929

Stock is a unit of ownership that people can buy in a company or business. Every stock has a specific money value. The stock market is where people can buy and sell their stocks. Before the stock market crash of 1929, stocks were worth a lot of money. People wanted to buy stocks, so they took out loans from banks to do so. Then the stock market "crashed," meaning that the prices of stocks fell dramatically. Many stocks that had been worth a lot of money were suddenly worthless. The people who owned those stocks, therefore, lost the money. People who had taken out loans to buy the stocks to begin with suddenly had no money to pay back those loans to the banks.

# World War II

Although the United States had been doing well in the 1920s, Germany had not. World War I had left Germany in economic ruin. Many Germans believed that only a strong leader could improve the country's condition. Adolf Hitler became that leader.

During the 1920s, Hitler and his ideas slowly grew in popularity. He blamed everyone except Germany for Germany's problems, including other countries and German Jews. He claimed that it was time for Germany to be a great power again. He formed the National Socialist German Workers group, or the Nazi Party, in 1920. By 1933, Hitler and his Nazis had great influence in Germany, and he was appointed chancellor (a powerful office under the president). Through a series of elections, Hitler then became the dictator of Germany. As dictator, Hitler had complete control over the country. People had to do as he said or face punishment.

The German people could not oppose Hitler in any way without the fear of being punished or even killed.

One of Hitler's primary goals was to strip all Jewish people in Germany of their rights, since he saw them as a major cause of Germany's problems. The anti-Semitism that had always existed in Europe reached an extreme level with Hitler in charge. When he became dictator, German Jews found themselves with no rights. They were not allowed to travel or go to school or practice their religion. But taking away these rights was just the first step. Hitler wanted Germany to be totally free of Jewish people, even if this meant killing them.

Ridding Germany of the Jewish people was not Hitler's only goal. Hitler wanted Germany to become a supreme power once again. He encouraged Austria to unite with Germany (Austria had become its own country after World War I in 1918), and then he invaded the Czech Republic

## A German Genius

One of the German Jewish immigrants to the United States in the 1930s was scientist Albert Einstein. Einstein was born in Ulm, Germany, in 1879. As a child, he was not always a good student. But as an adult, Einstein came up with several scientific theories that gained him notice around the world. In 1921, he won the Nobel Prize in physics. In 1932, Princeton University in New Jersey invited him to teach at its Institute for Advanced Study. Concerned about the growing anti-Jewish movement in Germany, Einstein came to the United States and lived in Princeton until his death in 1955.

and Slovakia. Germany also signed a treaty with Italy and Japan. (A treaty is an agreement made between two or more countries.) Germany, Italy, and Japan were now linked together by agreeing to support one another in case of war. When Germany invaded Poland in 1939, France and Great Britain declared war on Germany. This was the start of World War II (1939–1945).

Besides being allied with Germany, Japan wanted to be the supreme power in Asia. It began taking over lands in Asia by force. This angered the United States. After a few years of tense relations with the United States, Japan decided to strike. On December 7, 1941, Japanese warplanes bombed the American naval base at Pearl Harbor, Hawaii. The next day, the United States officially entered World War II by declaring war on Japan, and it declared war against Germany and Italy on December 11.

**UNITED STATES DEPARTMENT OF JUSTICE**

★

# NOTICE TO ALIENS OF ENEMY NATIONALITIES

★ The United States Government requires all aliens of German, Italian, or Japanese nationality to apply at post offices nearest to their place of residence for a Certificate of Identification. Applications must be filed between the period February 9 through February 28, 1942. *Go to your postmaster today for printed directions.*

FRANCIS BIDDLE,
*Attorney General.*

EARL G. HARRISON,
*Special Assistant to the Attorney General.*

## AVVISO

Il Governo degli Stati Uniti ordina a tutti gli stranieri di nazionalità Tedesca, Italiana e Giapponese di fare richiesta all' Ufficio Postale più prossimo al loro luogo di residenza per ottenere un Certificato d'Identità. Le richieste devono essere fatte entro il periodo che decorre tra il 9 Febbraio e il 28 Febbraio, 1942.
*Andate oggi dal vostro Capo d'Ufficio Postale (Postmaster) per ricevere le istruzioni scritte.*

## BEKANNTMACHUNG

Die Regierung der Vereinigten Staaten von Amerika fordert alle Auslaender deutscher, italienischer und japanischer Staatsangehoerigkeit auf, sich auf das ihrem Wohnorte naheliegende Postamt zu begeben, um einen Personalausweis zu beantragen. Das Gesuch muss zwischen dem 9. und 28. Februar 1942 eingereicht werden.
*Gehen Sie noch heute zu Ihrem Postmeister und verschaffen Sie sich die gedruckten Vorschriften.*

敵國外人注意

日獨伊諸國ノ國籍ヲ有スル在雷外人ハ
二月九日ヨリ二十八日マデノ間ニ其在所ニ二番
近イ郵便局デ自分ノ證明書ヲ申込ムコト可シ。
今日モ早速郵便局ヘ行キテ説明書ヲ賴ムヤウ願ヒマス。

**Post This Side In All States EXCEPT**
Arizona, California, Idaho, Montana, Nevada, Oregon, Utah, Washington

*During World War II, anti-immigrant sentiment was extremely high. This notice alerts all non-U.S. citizens of Japanese, German, and Italian descent to register their addresses with the government.*

During World War II, anti-German sentiment in the United States was not as strong as it had been in the previous war. This could be because many German Americans had become absorbed, or assimilated, into American society since World War I. Before World War I, many German Americans were proud of their background and openly followed German traditions. Because of anti-German sentiment during World War I, however, many German Americans hid their "German-ness." As a result, by the time of World War II, German-American culture was not as visible as it had been 20 years before.

# Internment Camps

During World War II, the United States was at war with Japan, Germany, and Italy. The U.S. government ordered some people in the United States who had Japanese, German, and Italian backgrounds to leave their homes and live in internment camps. Government leaders feared that these people might be more loyal to their homelands than to the United States. According to the government, these people might help their homelands in the war, thus causing harm to the United States. Confining Japanese, German, and Italian Americans in camps would prevent them from working against the United States. Most of the people in internment camps were Japanese Americans, who numbered 110,000 to 120,000. But from 3,000 to 10,000 German Americans were also interned.

The internment camps were nothing like summer camps. An internment camp was surrounded by fences and guard towers. People were crowded into hastily built barracks and had no privacy. They were forced to live there and not allowed to leave until the government said they could.

In December 1942, a camp in Crystal City, Texas, was opened. Thirty-five Germans and their families were the first to be housed there. At one point, Crystal City interned as many as 4,000 people, two-thirds of whom were Japanese.

# Escape from Nazi Germany

During Hitler's regime, between 1933 and 1945, Jews and other groups of Germans were persecuted by the Nazi government. As a result, many Germans fled their homeland in fear for their lives. Hitler's plan to rid his empire of Jews and other groups he considered "weak," including homosexuals and the disabled, resulted in the Holocaust, or the systematic rounding up and eventual killing of about 6 million people, most of them Jews. This killing took place mainly at death camps located throughout eastern Europe. As the Nazis spread out across Europe and people realized that their lives were in danger, no place felt safe unless it was an ocean away. About 130,000 Germans were able to escape from Germany and come to the United States.

What was Germany's loss became the United States' gain. Many of the people who emigrated before, during, and after the war were scientists, artists, writers, and musicians. Over the next decade, they would become successful Americans, adding to the achievements of the United States. ❈

Opposite: *A German family arrives in New York Harbor aboard the S.S. Nieuw Amsterdam. Families who were lucky enough to escape Germany during Hitler's rule found anti-German sentiment fading in America during the years following World War II.*

# Chapter Six

# A Continuing Legacy

*German Immigration from 1945 to Today*

# An Immigrant's Story

Two world wars had practically halted any interest in German culture in the United States. Even Americans who had German roots often did not acknowledge their past. But as the years passed, the memory of the prejudice suffered by German Americans began to fade. Although the wars could never be forgotten, Germany's involvement in those wars could be looked at objectively. People realized that even though Germany had been the United States' enemy during the war, German Americans and German culture were not the enemy. Slowly, German Americans once again began to embrace their German heritage.

*Most German immigrants have settled in these states.*

# A Divided Germany Once Again

When World War II ended in 1945, Germany was defeated. The armies of four countries occupied (remained in) Germany. Those countries were the United States, Great Britain, France, and the Soviet Union. Germany was divided into four sections. The Soviet Union, which had been an ally of the other three nations during the war, was now seen as a threat because it wanted to capture other countries and make them part of its Communist government. The section of Germany occupied by the Soviet Union became East Germany, which was a Communist country for many years. The remaining sections became the country of West Germany, or the Federal Republic of Germany.

In 1945, a young teenager named Thea Sobisch lived in the German city of Breslau. That year, when the war came to Breslau, Thea and her family were forced to leave. Eventually they settled in the town of Sonthofen in the German state of Bavaria. When the war was over, Thea began an apprenticeship to learn office skills, such as typing and note taking. The work, however, did not interest her.

Then, one day, a friend suggested that perhaps Thea could find work with an American military officer's family. After World War II, the American army had stayed behind in Germany. One of its goals was to make sure that Germany never again waged war against Europe. American soldiers lived in Germany, often with their families. They hired German people to look after their children and their households. In return, the Germans were given a place to live and food to eat in addition to their pay.

Thea found the idea appealing, and she soon found a job with an American military officer's family. She had taken some English classes in school before the war, but now she was able to learn English more thoroughly. She moved around with the family and enjoyed the Americans' easy ways. "I also learned a lot about American culture," she explained.

When the officer was transferred out of Germany, Thea began working at the American army base in Augsburg. There, she met and fell in love with an American soldier from New York City named Fred Trutkoff. Two months later, they were married.

Thea remembers sailing to America in early 1954. Her new husband had gone ahead of her, and she traveled by herself. "I wasn't frightened," she recalls. "The idea of going to the United States was exciting, it was something new."

*This photo shows two pages from the Hunold family passport.*
*This family traveled to Ellis Island in 1927 from*
*Heidenhein, Germany.*

On board the ship *Liberty*, Thea shared a room with another young woman. She recalls that the accommodations were a bit small—the room had bunk beds—but comfortable. The food was also good, and the ship itself was very clean and neat. Thea describes the trip as "fun": "There was music and dancing and games to play. Many young people were on the ship, and we had a great time." The crossing took eight days.

The most exciting moment of all was when the ship reached New York. "I stayed up all night to see the Statue of Liberty," Thea recalls. "I waited outside on the deck until it appeared. The sight was overwhelming. It's hard to explain."

Now, 50 years later, Thea Sobisch Trutkoff has no regrets about moving to America, even though she left her family behind. "I had a new life here. Soon we had a baby. I missed my parents and my brother, of course. But I was happy to be here." A few years after Thea arrived, she became an American citizen.

# A New Era of Immigration

The end of World War II did not see the end of Germans coming to live in America. Since 1950, about a million Germans have emigrated to the United States. Like Thea Sobisch, more than half a million came to the United States during the 1950s. The Great Depression in America had ended with the coming of the war, and work was not hard to find. Germany was not doing quite as well, and many Germans felt compelled to leave. Once again, America seemed like the place to go. It was a land of opportunities.

When World War II ended, the most powerful country in the world was not Germany, as Adolf Hitler had hoped. It was the United States. The United States had proven its military might during the war. At home, its citizens had proven their willingness to pull together and work hard, not for themselves, but for their country. The American economy grew stronger during the war.

Now, the U.S. government wanted to continue America's economic growth. Several plans were started to ensure America's prosperity. Workers' wages increased. The government helped people buy houses. The government also helped people who were out of work. The United States once again became a stable place to live.

Many Germans immigrated to the United States over the next several decades. Unlike the German immigrants of the past, many of the German immigrants of the mid-20th century did not cling to their traditions. As Thea Sobisch explained, "I wanted to be an American. I wanted to talk like Americans and dress like Americans. It never occurred to me to *not* try to be as American as I could."

# Contributions of New German Americans

M ost immigrants contribute something to their new home-land, whether it is their labor, their ideas, their arts, or many other things. Some immigrants make contributions that are more noticeable than others. This was especially true of German Americans. For example, two German Americans changed the appearance of American cities.

Walter Gropius (1883–1969) was born in Berlin. He became an architect. Gropius left Germany in 1934 after the Nazis came to power. He first lived in England, then came to the United States and became the head of the architecture department at Harvard University. In 1963, he designed an important building in New York City that was for many years known as the Pan Am Building.

Architect Ludwig Mies van der Rohe (1886–1969) was also born and educated in Germany. He arrived in the United States in 1937. He designed skyscrapers and other buildings in many cities, including the Seagram Building in New York. He is considered by many to be one of the three leading architects of the 20th century.

Thomas Mann (1875–1955) made his contribution through writing. He was born in Lubeck, Germany. One of his most important books is *Buddenbrooks*. It was published in Germany in 1901 and translated into English in 1904. Another well-known book is *The Magic Mountain*, which was written in 1924 and translated in 1927. Mann won the Nobel Prize for literature in 1929. He was opposed to the Nazi Party in Germany, and he lost his German citizenship in 1936. He lived in Switzerland for a while, then came to the United States in 1938. He became a United States citizen in 1944.

Another German American was important to the development of the space program in the United States. Wernher von Braun was born in Wirsitz, Germany, in 1912. He was fascinated by rockets from a very young age. During World War II, he was the director of the German Rocket Research Center. After the war, he was allowed to come to the United States to help the country develop its rocket program. He became a citizen in 1955. Five years later, he was an important figure at the National Aeronautics and Space Administration (NASA). Eventually he developed the *Saturn V* rocket that enabled American astronauts to land on the moon.

*The Seagram Building in New York City was designed by the German immigrant architect Mies van der Rohe. Van der Rohe is considered one of the most important architects of the 20th century.*

# Renewed German Pride

I t did not happen overnight. But slowly, German Americans began to acknowledge their cultural roots once more. German societies were formed. One of these was the German American National Congress. Founded in 1959, the group "seeks to bring together Americans of German descent in the pursuit of cultivating and presenting their heritage and interests on local, regional and national levels." In other words, the group's goal is to promote German culture in cities and towns across America.

Slowly, the evidence of America's German culture that had been erased during World War I was coming back. Statues of German Americans were once again erected. Classes in the German language were once again offered in schools. Music written by German composers was once again heard in concert halls. Some towns that had changed their German names during World War I even changed them back again.

# Celebrations

One example of the resurgence of German-American pride is the Steuben Parade. In the 1950s, several German Americans were concerned over the lack of German cultural awareness. After all, Germans had been one of the first groups of settlers in America. Germans had also helped the United States during the Revolution and the Civil War. Other cultures had parades to honor their nationalities, and German Americans felt that they should, too.

The founders of the parade decided to name it after the German military officer who helped George Washington during the Revolutionary War, Friedrich Wilhelm Augustin von Steuben. The first Steuben Parade was held in Queens, part of New York City, in 1957. In 1958, the parade marched down Fifth Avenue in Manhattan. It lasted about two hours, and more than 150,000 people showed up to enjoy it. Now, the parade is held every September in Manhattan and attracts more than half a million spectators.

*The Steuben Parade in New York City began in 1957, when German Americans wanted to raise the level of cultural awareness in America. These marchers from 1997 show their enthusiasm and traditional German dress.*

Throughout the year, German Americans also celebrate their cultural background at German fests. These gatherings are usually held outdoors and feature German music, German food, and German dancing. Men often wear lederhosen, the traditional suspenders and leather shorts of southern Germany, and women may wear the traditional dirndl dress and apron as they perform traditional dances. Everyone is invited to join in. Picnic tables are often set up under tents, and the atmosphere resembles a *biergarten* (beer garden) that one might find in Germany.

One of the biggest German fests in the United States is held each summer in Milwaukee, Wisconsin. It lasts for three days and attracts thousands of visitors. As the German Fest explains on its Web site: "This fun-filled, three-day weekend delivers nonstop entertainment with seven stages of German musicians and dance troupes from around the world, wonderful costume celebrations, contests, a live Glockenspiel and activities for the whole family." (The Glockenspiel is a famous clock in Munich that has moving figures.)

## German Food

Visitors to a German fest enjoy a variety of German foods. A sampling of those foods includes:

**bratwurst**—German sausage, usually brown in color

**weisswurst**—another German sausage, usually white in color

**schnitzel**—a thin piece of pork or veal, lightly breaded and fried

**sauerbraten**—a type of roast beef with gravy

**sauerkraut**—a shredded white cabbage dish

**strudel**—a fruit-filled pastry

# The United States and Germany Together

One of the reasons that German Americans are once again embracing their heritage could be that the United States and Germany have a good relationship. Many products from the United States are exported to Germany, and likewise, many German products are imported into the United States.

Some of the most popular German products are cars. Several well-known car manufacturers have their roots firmly in Germany. Volkswagen is a German company, as are Mercedes and Audi. BMW automobiles are also German. The letters stand for Bavarian Motor Works. The export of German cars to the United States makes up about one-fourth of all exported German products.

In addition, the U.S. Army still maintains bases in Germany. Germany and the United States both contribute money to keep these bases operating. One base includes the Landstuhl Regional Medical Center. It is the largest American hospital outside the United States.

# German-American Culture

Germans have been an important part of American culture for more than 300 years. It would be difficult to imagine the United States without German influences. In fact, many customs that are considered American have their roots in German tradition.

For example, many Christmas traditions come from Germany. Decorating a tree for Christmas is a German tradition. German Protestants were also the first to give gifts on December 25. Groundhog Day, celebrated each February 2, also comes from a German tradition, in which farmers would predict the arrival of spring by checking to see if a groundhog saw its shadow.

Many well-known children's stories also come from Germany. Jacob Ludwig Karl Grimm and Wilhelm Karl Grimm were brothers. They collected folktales told throughout Germany. Today many of those stories are called Grimms' fairy tales. "Hansel and Gretel," "Snow White and the Seven

Dwarfs," and "Sleeping Beauty" are just a few of the German folktales that were preserved by the Grimm brothers.

# Into the Next Century

Germany is now a stable country, and people do not feel the need to emigrate as they once did. Even so, German people still make the trip to the United States, and many decide to stay. According to the U.S. Citizenship and Immigration Service, between 1989 and 2002 more than 100,000 Germans immigrated to the United States—a little more than 7,200 per year. This number, however, is relatively small when compared to other immigrant groups. In 2002, the total number of all legal immigrants to the United States was 1,063,732. The number of Germans who immigrated that year was 8,961. That number is less than 1 percent of all immigrants in 2002.

Helga Hill immigrated to the United States in 1988. Originally from a town in Bavaria on the Danube River, she explains that she met her husband, Stephen, in Germany at a party. "He is American, but his family is from the same town as me." Soon Helga was making wedding plans—and plans to move to the United States.

She recalls her feelings as she flew in an airplane to meet her future husband. "I felt everything at once. I was excited, but I was also a little naïve. I didn't think the separation from my friends and family [in Germany] would be so difficult."

Life became quite busy for Helga and Stephen when the first of five children came along. Because Helga is German, her children are considered first-generation Americans. Helga and Stephen Hill have introduced their children to their German background. The Hills frequently attend German fests near their home in New Jersey. They also try to see the Steuben Parade in New

# Speaking German

Some German words have become a familiar part of the English language.

**angst:** a strong feeling of fear or anxiety

**blitz:** a play in football in which players try to tackle the quarterback; in German, *blitzen* means "lightning"

**frankfurter:** a sausage eaten on a roll; named after Frankfurt, Germany

**gesundheit:** something one says after someone sneezes; translated, it means, "Good health!"

**hamburger:** a meat patty served on a roll; named after Hamburg, Germany

**kaput:** finished, broken, or destroyed

**poltergeist:** a ghost that makes a lot of noise; in German, *poltern* means "to knock," and a *geist* is a ghost or a spirit

**rottweiler:** a breed of dog, named after the town of Rottweil, Germany

**spritz:** a sprinkle or a small spray; in German, *spritzen* means "to sprinkle"

**Volkswagen:** a brand of car made in Germany; translated, the word *volks* means "folks," and *wagen* means "car" or "wagon"

**waltz:** a type of dance

**yodel:** a type of singing or calling; in German, this word is spelled *jodeln* (the letter *j* is pronounced like the English letter *y*)

York City every year. Although Helga does not speak much German at home, her children are very aware and proud of their German background.

*German immigrant Rudolf Stember has designed computer music and sound effects for more than 100 video games. He is shown holding two Star Wars models.*

As life in America has changed over the last 300 years, so have German immigrants. Most early German settlers were farmers and craftspeople. By comparison, only about 1 percent of German immigrants who come to the United States today are farmers. Craftspeople make up a little more than 10 percent of German immigrants. On the other hand, one-third of German immigrants who work in the United States are business managers, while another third have technical jobs. A little more than 13 percent of German immigrants in the workforce have jobs in the service industries, such as restaurants and hotels.

From their earliest sailings to the colonies, German Americans have left their mark on America. And with one in every four Americans claiming to have German ancestors, it is little wonder that German-American pride has returned. In fact, the 1990 census revealed that German Americans were the largest ethnic group in 29 states. The presence of German Americans might not be felt as strongly as that of other immigrant groups, largely because German culture and tradition have become part of American culture. Yet the German presence in America can still be felt and appreciated by looking at America's history and by examining the very fabric of American life.

# Time Line of German Immigration

1400s     Germany is made up of more than 200 individual states, each with its own ruler.

1517     Martin Luther speaks out against the Roman Catholic Church. The Reformation begins.

1618–1648     The Thirty Years' War is fought in Europe, mostly on German lands. German states are left in ruins.

1683     First major group of German immigrants arrives in Philadelphia, Pennsylvania, on October 6. They became known as the Krefelders, after the town from which they came. Along with Francis Daniel Pastorius, they settle the town of Germantown, Pennsylvania.

1727     German immigrants to America must swear allegiance to England.

1732     The first German newspaper in America is published in Philadelphia.

1749–1754     About 37,000 Germans arrive at the port of Philadelphia.

1756–1763     The Seven Years' War is fought, involving the colonies, England, France, and other European countries.

1775     The Revolutionary War begins.

1778     Baron von Steuben, a German army officer, trains George Washington's troops at Valley Forge, Pennsylvania.

1783     The Revolutionary War ends. German immigrants are the largest group of non-English immigrants in the United States.

1806     Napoleon Bonaparte, the emperor of France, conquers many of the German states. He is defeated in 1815.

1812     The War of 1812 begins in the United States.

1815     Wars in Europe and the United States end. Immigration from Germany begins again.

| | |
|---|---|
| 1833 | The Giessen Emigration Society is established to encourage people from Germany to come to the United States. Although it does not last, it is the first of many such societies. |
| 1848 | Uprisings and revolts in the German states force many Germans to leave Europe and come to the United States. These German immigrants are called the "Forty-Eighters." |
| 1856 | Margarethe Meyer Schurz starts the first kindergarten in the United States. |
| 1861–1865 | The American Civil War is fought. |
| 1862 | Congress passes the Homestead Act. |
| 1870s | Russian Germans begin to arrive in the Midwest, bringing a new type of wheat with them. |
| 1871 | Germany becomes one country, ruled by Wilhelm I. |

| | |
|---|---|
| 1890 | About 2.8 million German-born immigrants live in the United States. Wilhelm II, also known as Kaiser Wilhelm, is the ruler of Germany. |
| 1914–1918 | World War I is fought. |
| 1915 | A German submarine sinks the *Lusitania*, a British passenger ship. |
| 1929 | The American stock market crashes and the Great Depression begins. |
| 1939–1945 | World War II is fought. When the war is over, Germany becomes two countries, East Germany and West Germany. |

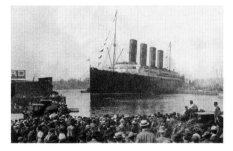

| | |
|---|---|
| 1950s | Half a million Germans come to live in the United States. |
| 1957 | The first Steuben Parade is held to honor German Americans. In 1958, it is held in Manhattan, where it has been held every year since. |
| 1983 | The tricentennial of the Krefelders' immigration to Pennsylvania is celebrated. |
| 1987 | German-American Day is officially established by President Ronald Reagan. |
| 1990 | Germany is once again a unified country. |
| 2002 | Over half a million people attend the Steuben Parade in Manhattan. |

# Glossary

**assimilate** To absorb or blend into the way of life of a society.

**culture** The language, arts, traditions, and beliefs of a society.

**democratic** Governed by the majority rule of the people.

**emigrate** To leave one's homeland to live in another country.

**ethnic** Having certain racial, national, tribal, religious, or cultural origins.

**guild** Group of people with common interests, such as shop owners or craftspeople.

**immigrate** To come to a foreign country to live.

**internment** Imprisonment, especially during a time of war.

**Krefelders** Group of people who came from Germany to America in 1683. Usually considered the first group of German immigrants.

**labor union** Organization that fights for workers' rights, such as better pay and working conditions.

**Nazi** a member of the National Socialist German Workers' party, which ruled Germany during World War II and was headed by Adolf Hitler.

**neutral** Not favoring one side or another during a time of war.

**Pennsylvania Dutch** German people living in Pennsylvania. *Dutch* is a mispronunciation of *Deutsch*, the German word for "German."

**prejudice** Negative opinion formed without just cause.

**principality** Territory of a prince or other ruler.

**Reformation** Religious movement in Europe in the 1500s, marked by the establishment of Protestant churches.

**refugee** Someone who flees a place for safety reasons, especially to another country.

# Further Reading

## BOOKS

Ashbrock, Peg. *The German Americans*. Philadelphia: Mason Crest, 2003.

Frost, Helen. *German Immigrants, 1820–1920*. Mankato, Minn.:
    Blue Earth Books, 2002.

Galicich, Anne. *The German Americans*. New York: Chelsea House, 2001.

Gurasich, Marj. *Letters to Oma: A Young Girl's Account of Her First Year in
    Texas, 1847*. Fort Worth: Texas Christian University Press, 1989.

Parker, Lewis K. *Why German Immigrants Came to America*. New York:
    PowerKids Press, 2003.

## WEB SITES

The German Americans. "An Ethnic Experience." URL:
    www.ulib.iupui.edu/kade/adams/toc.html. Downloaded on
    June 29, 2004.

German Embassy, Washington, D.C. "German-Americans." URL:
    www.germany-info.org/relaunch/culture/ger_americans/
    ger_americans.html. Downloaded on June 29, 2004.

History of German-American Relations. "1683–1900 History and
    Immigration." URL: www.usembassy.de/usa/garelations8300.htm.
    Downloaded on June 29, 2004.

Thinkquest. "Immigration: The Journey to America–the Germans." URL:
    http://library.thinkquest.org/20619/German.html. Downloaded on
    June 29, 2004.

# Index